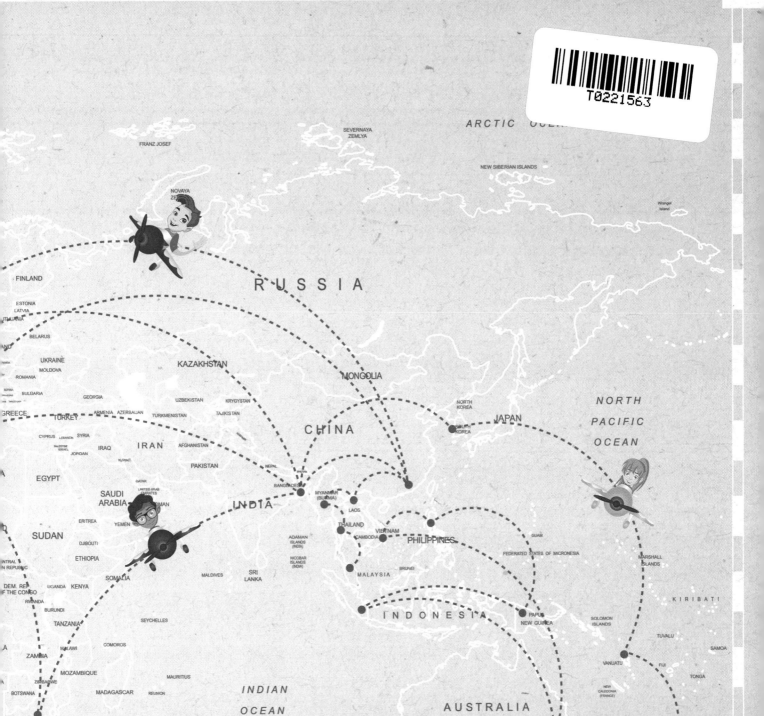

GLOBETROTTERS

# PACIFIC ISLANDS

Jane Hinchey

REDBACK
publishing

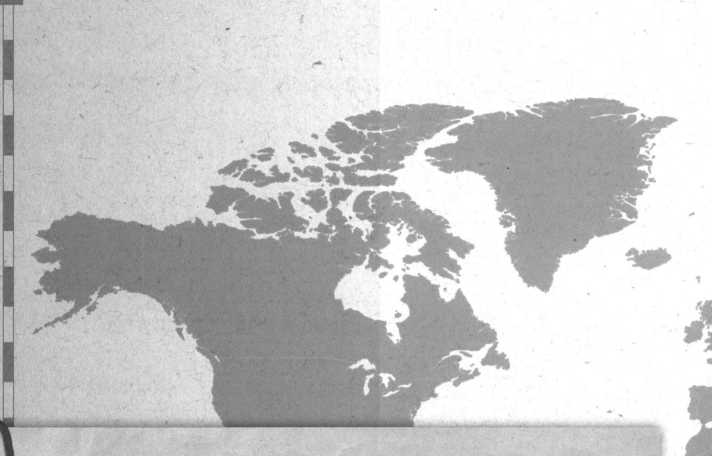

First Published 2022 by
Redback Publishing
PO Box 357 Frenchs Forest NSW 2086
Australia

www.redbackpublishing.com
orders@redbackpublishing.com

ISBN 978-1-922322-32-6

Author: Jane Hinchey
Editor: Marlene Vaughan
Design: Redback Publishing

Original illustrations © Redback Publishing 2022
Originated by Redback Publishing

Printed and bound in Malaysia

Acknowledgements
Abbreviations: l—left, r—right, b—bottom, t—top, c—centre, m—middle
We would like to thank the following for permission to reproduce photographs:
(Images © shutterstock, wikimediacommons) p8bl ChameleonsEye, p13tl Laszlo Mates,
p13mr Laszlo Mates, p16bl Ignacio Moya Coronado, p18tc Julie Lyn (https://commons.
wikimedia.org/wiki/File:Fiji_(9473930207)_(2).jpg), p19tr Simi Tukidia (https://commons.
wikimedia.org/wiki/File:Coat_of_arms_of_Fiji.svg), p19mr Guy Cowdry, p21tr Katja
Tsvetkova, p21ml Ikonya, p22br ausnewsde, p25ml Laszlo Mates, p26tl Don Mammoser, p27tr
Unknown author (https://commons.wikimedia.org/wiki/File:Salote_Tupou_III_in_her_
coronation_robe_seated_outside_with_her_consort.jpg), p27ml Unknown author (https://
commons.wikimedia.org/wiki/File:Salote_Tupou_III_of_Tonga_in_1908.jpg), p28tr
Wirestock Creators, p28bl THP Creative, p29bl Louis Triquéra (https://commons.wikimedia.
org/wiki/File:Stamp_New_Caledonia_1860_single.jpg), p29br Clement Lindley Wragge
(https://commons.wikimedia.org/wiki/File:The_Prison_Canaque,_New_Caledonia,_
Outside_the_Walls.jpg), p30tl Ritu Manoj Jethani, p30mr New Zealand Government, Office
of the Governor-General, CC BY 4.0 (https://commons.wikimedia.org/wiki/File:Albert_
Wendt_ONZ_investiture.jpg), p31tr Public domain (https://commons.wikimedia.org/wiki/
File:1964_-_Boyd_Theater_-_12_Feb_MC_-_Allentown_PA.jpg), p31ml Reynold Brown
(https://commons.wikimedia.org/wiki/File:Poster_for_Mutiny_on_the_Bounty.jpg), p31br
Lloyd Osbourne (https://commons.wikimedia.org/wiki/File:Robert_Louis_Stevenson_with_
Princess_Liliuokalani,_c._1889,_PBA_Galleries.jpg), p32tr hyotographics

Disclaimer
All the internet addresses (URLs) given in this book were valid at the time of going to press.
However, due to the dynamic nature of the internet, some addresses may have changed, or
sites may have changed or ceased to exist since publication. While the author and publisher
regret any inconvenience this may cause readers, no responsibility for any such changes can be
accepted by either the author or the publisher.

A catalogue record for this
book is available from the
National Library of Australia

# CONTENTS

The Rock Islands
PALAU

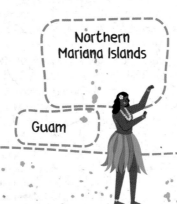

Northern Mariana Islands

Wake Island

Marshall Islands

Guam

Palau

The Federated States of Micronesia

Papua New Guinea

Nauru

Solomon Islands

Coral Sea Islands

Vanuatu

New Caledonia

AUSTRALIA

Sri Siva Subramaniya Temple
FIJI

Baining Firework Dance
PAPUA NEW GUINEA

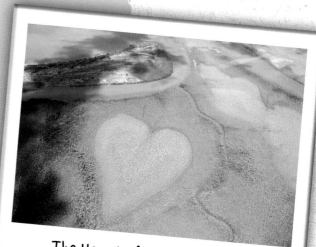
The Heart of Voh mangroves
NEW CALEDONIA

# MAP OF THE PACIFIC ISLANDS

Mo'orea
FRENCH POLYNESIA

Kiribati

Tuvalu

Tokelau

Wallis and Futuna

Samoa

American Samoa

Cook Islands

Tonga

Fiji

Niue

French Polynesia

Pitcairn Islands

## The Pacific Islands

There are thousands of islands in the Pacific Islands which are spread across 15 per cent of the Earth's surface and represent numerous diverse cultures and languages. Pacific Islanders speak nearly a quarter of the world's languages.

# INTRODUCING THE PACIFIC ISLANDS

There are three separate regions in the Pacific, reflecting the linguistics, culture and ethnic backgrounds of the indigenous people who live there, as well as the geography of the islands.

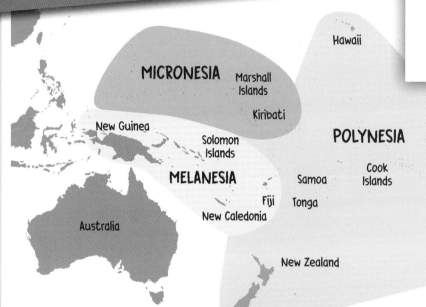

MICRONESIA

Marshall Islands

Kiribati

Hawaii

New Guinea

Solomon Islands

POLYNESIA

MELANESIA

Samoa

Tonga

Cook Islands

Fiji

New Caledonia

Australia

Easter Island

New Zealand

## Delicious Fact
Sugar cane probably originated in the South Pacific.

Harvesting sugar cane on Viti Levu island in Fiji

# Melanesia

Melanesia is a vast area of approximately one million square kilometres, located north and east of Australia. It consists of about 2,000 islands, many of them have been inhabited for tens of thousands of years. Melanesia includes the islands of Fiji, New Guinea, the Solomon Islands, Vanuatu, New Caledonia and the Torres Strait Islands.

# Polynesia

Polynesia is the largest region in the Pacific Islands and includes countries such as Tonga, the Cook Islands, Niue, Easter Island, Western Samoa, American Samoa, French Polynesia and Pitcairn Island.

Polynesian hula dancers with fire torches

# Micronesia

Micronesia means small islands. It is a chain of about 2,500 mostly small, flat islands. The whole region is warm and wet, with average annual temperatures ranging between 20 and 30 degrees. Kiribati, Guam, Nauru and the Marshall Islands are all in Micronesia.

Majuro atoll and city in the Marshall islands

The Pacific Islands region is spread across a vast area of the Earth, encompassing a diverse range of geographical and marine ecosystems, and tremendous biodiversity. There are volcanic islands and low coral atolls. Both Australia and New Zealand are part of the Pacific.

# GEOGRAPHY AND CLIMATE

Farm workers harvest the pineapple crop in Polynesia

## Climate

As they are located between the Tropic of Cancer and the Tropic of Capricorn, the climate of the Pacific Islands is generally tropical. The summer months are November to April; this is also cyclone season in the area. The winter months of April to October are only slightly cooler.

Cyclones are common between April and October

## High Islands

High islands are preferable habitats for settlement, as they have abundant fresh water. Volcanic islands have fertile soil, perfect for farming, and most are covered with tropical forests.

These islands are created when underwater volcanos erupt and increase in height over time. The high islands of the Pacific are found mainly in Polynesia and Melanesia.

Uninhabited island in Chuuk, Micronesia

Coral and double-saddle Butterflyfish, Huahine island, French Polynesia

# Coral Atolls

An atoll, or low island, is a coral reef that encircles a lagoon. It first develops when an underwater volcano erupts, creating an island. The next stage is when corals build a reef around the island. Over millions of years, the ocean erodes parts of the reef creating sand, where plants grow. Coral only grows in warm water, so coral atolls are found only in tropical latitudes. As they are low-lying with infertile soil, most atolls are uninhabited. These low islands are found mainly in Micronesia and Polynesia.

## Seriously Cool

The Pacific Islands have more than 25 species of birds of paradise.

# Who named the Pacific Ocean?

In October 1520, Ferdinand Magellan sailed into the Pacific Ocean from the more treacherous Atlantic Ocean, becoming the first European explorer to do so. He found the ocean so calm by comparison, that he named it 'Pacifico' from the Latin word pacificus, meaning 'tranquil.' The Pacific Ocean is the largest, deepest ocean on Earth, covering more than 30 per cent of the world's surface.

# The Ring of Fire

The Ring of Fire is located in the Pacific region, which means the area is prone to earthquakes and volcanic activity. Three-quarters of the world's volcanoes are located here, as well as much of the world's seismic activity.

Ring of Fire

Indo-Australian Plate

**Mount Yasur erupting, Tanna Island**
VANUATU

**Mount Yasur volcano, Tanna Island**
VANUATU

Australia, New Guinea, Fiji and part of New Zealand are located on the Indo-Australian Plate, while the northern and central Pacific sit on the Pacific Plate. The Mariana Trench, the deepest point on earth, is in the Western Pacific.

High islands are usually volcanic in origin. Low-lying islands, or atolls, are generally composed of coral.

# PACIFIC ISLANDS FORUM

The Pacific Islands Forum is an inter-governmental organisation that fosters relationships between countries in the Pacific Ocean. However, there are tensions between Australia and many of these small nations due to Australia's environmental policies. Australia, along with New Zealand, are the two wealthiest countries in the region, with carbon-polluting industries that contribute to climate change in the region.

The 13 member states of the Pacific Forum are:
- Australia
- Cook Islands
- Fiji
- French Polynesia
- New Caledonia
- New Zealand
- Niue
- Papua New Guinea
- Samoa
- Solomon Islands
- Tonga
- Tuvalu
- Vanuatu

After disagreements in 2021, the following five states will cease their membership in February 2022:
- The Federated States of Micronesia
- Kiribati
- Marshall Islands
- Nauru
- Palau

The Pacific Islands are vulnerable to severe weather, rising sea levels and flooding, which leads to crops being poisoned by seawater. Pacific Island leaders have called for a move away from coal, something Australia refuses to do, causing tension in the region.

# PROBLEMS IN THE PACIFIC

The Pacific Island nations face a number of threats, such as deforestation and overfishing. Countries around the infamous Ring of Fire are at risk from volcanoes and earthquakes. Along with the devastation earthquakes can cause, there are also the associated risks, such as landslides and tsunamis.

Many of the Pacific Islands are particularly vulnerable to climate change. Ocean temperatures are rising and coastal areas have suffered from erosion. Five uninhabited islands belonging to the Solomon Island chain are now underwater. A number of other islands have already suffered with villages and farmlands being swept into the sea. The islands are vulnerable to severe cyclones and flash foods.

With the impact of climate change being felt on many islands, so too are associated health problems. There is a rise in vector-borne diseases, caused by mosquitoes, bugs, sandflies and flies. There is also a rise in respiratory illnesses, eye disease and psychological issues.

## TALK ABOUT IT

The main threats to Pacific Islanders that can be attributed to climate change are:
- Rising sea levels
- Destructive weather
- Health issues

Can you name any other threats associated with climate change?

A UN report shows that many Pacific Islanders are already leaving their homes and heading to Australia, New Zealand or Fiji.

As extreme weather due to climate change increases, more people are expected to leave their island homes.

# FIJI IN FOCUS

Traditional Fijian houses in Navala village in the Ba Highlands of northern-central Viti Levu, Fiji

Fiji is an island country in the South Pacific. It takes between four and five hours to fly to Fiji from the east coast of Australia. Fiji is an archipelago spread over an area of about 1.3 million square kilometres. It has 333 islands of which just over 100 are inhabited, and more than 500 islets. The capital Suva is located on the island of Viti Levu, where 75 per cent of the population live. Fiji is rich with resources, so has one of the Pacific's strongest economies.

## Education

Education is free for children between the ages of six and sixteen. There are a range of schools, from government schools to Catholic, Methodist and Muslim schools. Fijian and Indo-Fijian children attend separate schools. Fiji has a 93 per cent literacy rate.

## Local Lingo: Fijian

**Ni sa yadra**
Good morning

**Bula**
Welcome

**Vinaka**
Thank you

**Vacava tiko?**
How are you?

# The People

Fiji's population is 54 per cent native Fijian, descending from Melanesian and Polynesian backgrounds. Another 38 per cent of Fiji's population is Indo (Indian)-Fijian. These two groups have a history of tension. Even those of Indian descent whose family have lived in Fiji for generations aren't called Fijian. Only indigenous Fijians can claim this title.

Indo-fijian celebrating a festival at Sri Siva Subramaniya Temple, Fiji

There are smaller populations of other Pacific Islanders, Chinese and Europeans. Extended families live together and, when a couple marry, the two families view each other as family as well. Clans or family groups own about 85 per cent of land. Indo-Fijians are not allowed to own land.

## SNAPSHOT

**COUNTRY**
Republic of Fiji

**CAPITAL**
Suva

**OFFICIAL LANGUAGES**
English (official), Fijian (official), Hindustani

**AREA**
18,274 square kilometres

**POPULATION**
903,274 (2021)

**ETHNIC GROUPS**
Indigenous Fijian 54%, Indo-Fijian 38%

**RELIGIONS**
Christian, Hindu, a small Muslim population

**CURRENCY**
FJ$ Fijian dollar

**GOVERNMENT**
Fiji is a republic. All citizens vote. The Great Council of Chiefs deals with traditional matters.

# FIJI'S HISTORY

Fiji was settled between 3500 and 1000 BC. While Fijian legend says that the great chief Lutunasobasoba led his people across the seas to the new land of Fiji, the first people actually arrived from Southeast Asia via the Malay Peninsula. These original inhabitants were the Lapita people, named after the type of pottery they produced. The first European to spot Fiji was Abel Tasman in 1643, followed by James Cook over 100 years later.

Vanua Levu, Fiji islands. Created by De Bar after Williams, published in Le Tour du Monde, Paris, 1860

However, the first Europeans to live there were shipwrecked sailors and escaped convicts from Australia. In the mid-1800s, traders and missionaries arrived. In 1874, Fiji became a British colony, and then a republic in 1987.

## Cheers!

An important part of every village ceremony is the sharing of a drink called yaquona (kava) from a carved bowl.

# TOURISM AND TRADE

*Basket weaving lesson using coconut palm leaves*

## Traditional Crafts

Weaving and woodcarving remain popular traditions in Fiji today. Girls are taught weaving from a young age, using flax, coconut palms or pandanus trees to make mats, bags and hats. These are popular with tourists.

## Tourism

One of Fiji's major industries is tourism. Visitor arrivals for 2019 totalled 900,000. This was an increase of 4.2 per cent compared to the year before.

## Trading Partners:

Fiji's principal export destinations are the USA, Australia and the UK, while its top three import sources are Singapore, Australia and New Zealand.

## Top Exports:

Coconut oil, raw sugar, timber, fish, mineral water, ginger, flour and taro.

## Top Imports:

Refined petroleum, planes, cars and fish.

# FLAG, SYMBOLS AND EMBLEMS

## Flag Of Fiji

Fiji's flag has a blue background, symbolic of the Pacific Ocean. It bears a coat of arms showing a golden lion holding a cocoa pod, as well as panels displaying a palm tree, sugar cane, bananas and a dove of peace. In the top left corner is the Union Jack, which symbolises Fiji's long association with Great Britain. This flag has been in use since October 10, 1970.

# Coat of Arms

Two Fijian warriors stand either side of a shield containing the Cross of St. George. The lion at the top of the shield represents the United Kingdom, while the dove represents peace. The images of the sugarcane, bananas and coconut palm are symbolic of Fiji's resources. Above the shield is a traditional canoe, while underneath is Fiji's motto: 'Fear God and honour the Queen'.

# Special Days

Fiji celebrates numerous public holidays throughout the year, including local and regional ones. Some of the more important national holidays include:

- Fiji Day – this October holiday commemorates the 1970 end of British colonial rule.

- Hibiscus Festival – held in Fiji's capital city every August, this is a fun-filled family festival.

# National Anthem

The National Anthem is *Meda Dau Doka* or *God Bless Fiji*. Although there are English and Fijian versions of the anthem, they are not direct translations and are quite different.

# WELCOME TO VANUATU

Vanuatu is a Y-shaped archipelago of over 80 islands, stretching north from the Tropic of Capricorn. It has risen 700 metres from the sea in the past 3 million years and is still rising a millimetre a year.

## Fast Fact

Vanuatu has 150 species of orchid

All the islands of Vanuatu have their own rich customs and languages. The official languages of Vanuatu are French, English and Bislama, which is a creole language. There are also 105 other local languages spoken in Vanuatu. Vanuatu is a popular holiday destination for Australians looking for the perfect tropical getaway. Also popular are cruises that include Vanuatu in their itinerary.

## Local Lingo: Bislama

**Yu toktok Engglis?**
Do you speak English?

**Alo**
Hello

**Tata**
Goodbye

**Wanem nem blong you?**
What's your name?

## Education

Literacy rates in Vanuatu are among the lowest in the South Pacific. Education is compulsory up until the age of twelve, but only a third of children continue after this.

# The People

The people of Vanuatu are called ni-Vanuatu and are of Melanesian descent. Ni-Vanuatu make up 98 per cent of the population, with smaller groups from Australia, France, New Zealand, Vietnam and China. The majority of ni-Vanuatu live in villages, where family life is the priority. Extended families live together and the elders teach the children their traditional ways.

Ni-Vanuatu in traditional clothing, Tanna, Vanuatu

## Religion

Christianity is the main religion of Vanuatu and it has been incorporated into the local folklore and spiritual traditions. Ancestor worship and communication with spirits is as much a part of daily life as Christian practices.

## Pass the Salt!

Did you know that the first missionaries to arrive on Vanuatu were eaten?

## SNAPSHOT

**COUNTRY**

Republic of Vanuatu

**CAPITAL**

Port Vila

**OFFICIAL LANGUAGES**

Bislama, English, French

**AREA**

12,189 square kilometres

**POPULATION**

302,120 (2019)

**CURRENCY** VT Vanuatu Vatu (VUV)

**RELIGIONS** Christian, Presbyterian, Catholic and Anglican

# VANUATU TIMELINE

**1500 BC**
Lapita people arrive, followed by other settlers from Melanesia and Polynesia

**1200**
Chief Roi Mata unites the tribes and rules peacefully, until poisoned by his brother

**1606**
Portuguese explorer, Pedro Fernandez de Quiros, is the first European to land on Vanuatu

**1774**
Captain Cook charts the islands and calls them New Hebrides

**1839**
European missionaries arrive, bringing Christianity. Sandalwood traders and settlers also arrive and begin farming cotton, cocoa and cattle

**1906–1980**
Britain and France jointly govern

**1980**
Vanuatu becomes a republic on July 30

**2015**
Cyclone Pam, a Category 5 cyclone, devastates many of the islands

**Fast Fact**
Vanuatu means 'Land Eternal.'

Cyclone Pam destroyed about 80 per cent of Vanuatu's buildings

## Government

Both France and Britain ruled over Vanuatu (New Hebrides) for 74 years. It resulted in two systems of schooling, courts, hospitals and police being introduced to Vanuatu. Since independence in 1980, a president is elected for a five-year term. The general public elects members of Parliament to four-year terms. There is also a Council of Chiefs that oversees customs and traditions.

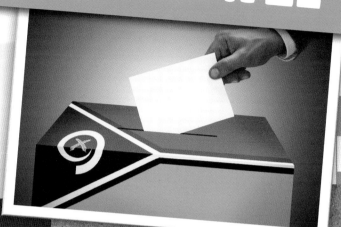

## Top Exports:
Copra, frozen fish, beef, coffee, timber, cocoa and pepper.

## Top Imports:
Passenger and cargo ships, refined petroleum and food products.

## Transport

Vanuatu has no railway and its roads are underdeveloped. There is no public transport system in Vanuatu. It's common to see mini buses hurtling down the roads and these can be flagged down like taxis. These mini buses are privately owned. Each island has a port and an airstrip and Vanuatu is a popular destination for cruise ships.

# VANUATU'S FLAG, SYMBOLS AND EMBLEMS

## Coat of Arms

The Vanuatu coat of arms shows a Melanesian warrior holding a spear, standing before a mountain. Behind him are a boar's tusk and two namele fern fronds. At the base of the image is a scroll that says 'Long God Yumi Stanap' in Bislama, which means 'In God We Stand.'

The flag of Vanuatu was officially adopted on Independence Day, July 30, 1980.

## Flag Of Vanuatu

Vanuatu is a chain of islands in the shape of a Y, and the yellow horizontal Y, bordered in black, is representative of this. Yellow symbolizes sunshine, while green is symbolic of the lush lands. Red symbolises the sacred pig's blood that is important in traditional religious ceremonies. The Black triangle holds an image of a pig's tusk.'

# Special Days

Vanuatu celebrates numerous public holidays throughout the year, including local and regional ones. Some of the more important national holidays include:

- Independence Day – a July holiday commemorating the 1980 end of British and French rule.

- Nagol Land Diving Festival – every Saturday between April and June, men perform a rite of passage by (bungee) jumping from 30-metre high stick towers using vines.

Hibiscus, Vanuatu's national flower

Rom dancers and a village chief perform a magical dance at the edge of the rainforest

## North Ambrym Magic Festival

Each July, magicians and sorcerers come out to celebrate and demonstrate their magic and spirit-summoning skills. The yam, an important food in Vanuatu, is also honoured through stories, which teach how to grow, harvest and eat the yam.

## National Anthem

Since 1980, the national anthem has been *Yumi, Yumi, Yumi*, meaning *We, We, We.*

# GREETINGS FROM TONGA

Fire dance in Hina cave, Tongatapa, Tonga

## The Kingdom of Tonga

Tonga consists of 170 islands running in two lines. Tonga has a population of 106,326 people, spread across 36 of these islands. The islands in the eastern chain are coral atolls. The islands are divided into three groups: Tongatapu group, Ha'apai group and Vava'u group.

Tonga has been inhabited for about 3000 years. The first European to visit Tonga was Dutch navigator, Jakob Le Maire, in 1616. He was followed by Abel Tasman in 1643, then by Captain James Cook, who named Tonga the Friendly Islands.

Tonga is the only monarchy in the Pacific. The Tongan monarchy has existed since the 10th century. The country's capital is Nuku'alofa.

## Traditional Tongan Food

Ota ika is a traditional dish, often served before meals. It consists of raw fish soaked in lime juice, coconut milk and chilli peppers. Other popular dishes are chicken wrapped in banana leaves and cooked in coconut milk, and fish or lobsters served with taro leaves. During Tongan celebrations such as weddings and funerals, meals are cooked in an underground oven called an umu.

Ota ika

# Tonga Timeline

Queen Salote Tupou III (right)

**1000 BC**
The seafaring Lapita people arrive

**950 AD**
The Tu'i Tonga empire

**1773-1777**
James Cook visits and names Tonga the Friendly Islands

**1797**
English missionaries arrive

**1845**
Tāufa'āhau Tupou becomes King and changes his name to King George Tupou I

**1900**
Tonga signs a treaty with Britain and becomes a British protectorate

**1918-1965**
Queen Salote rules

**1970**
Tonga becomes independent from Britain

**1999**
Tonga joins the United Nations

Queen Salote Tupou III reigned for 48 years, until her death in 1965. The people of Tonga mourned this great Queen when she died. She came to the throne when she was 18 and was considered to be a kind and clever ruler.

Queen Salote Tupou III of Tonga at age eight in 1908

## Fast Fact

All children between six and fourteen are legally required to attend school. State-run schools are free, but churches run many of the high schools and they charge fees. The main languages are Tongan and English.

# WELCOME TO NEW CALEDONIA

This French territory is situated 2,000 kilometres north-east of Sydney. It has a population of about 288,474 people. Indigenous Kanaks make up 45 per cent while approximately 30 per cent are of French descent. French is the official language, however about 30 other indigenous languages are also spoken.

The French President is head of state but a locally-elected Territorial Congress and President govern. While it is still a French colony, around 43 per cent of citizens want independence.

## Three Fast Facts:

**1.** About 10 per cent of the world's known nickel resources are in New Caledonia

**2.** The Belize Barrier Reef is the second longest double barrier reef in the world

**3.** New Caledonia boasts the world's largest lagoon

# Convict Past

New Caledonia has a convict past. After New Caledonia was claimed by the French in in 1853, 20,000 convicts were sentenced to transportation to the new colony between 1864 and 1897.

Remains of the prison in Prony, New Caledonia

# New Caledonia Timeline

**1500-1000 BC**
Lapita people arrive

**1000-1700**
Polynesian settlers arrive

**1774**
Captain Cook names the island New Caledonia

**1840s**
Christian missionaries arrive

**1853**
France claims New Caledonia

**1864-1897**
French convicts are sent to the island

**1888**
New Caledonia becomes a self-ruling territory of France

**1894**
French settlers start arriving

**1946**
Kanaks made French citizens

A copy of the first New Caledonia stamp (1860), reprinted from the original plate

Outside the prison in Canaque, New Caledonia

# LITERATURE

Performance at Polynesian Cultural Centre in Oahu, Hawaii

## Oral Traditions

Pacific Islanders passed down stories through the generations, using oral traditions. These included myths, legends, family and local stories, religious tales and traditions, passed on using narrative, song and dance and choral performance. Oral traditions in the Pacific Islands remain strong and stories continue to be created, performed and exchanged.

## The Written Tale

One of the most prolific writers from the region is Albert Wendt. Born in Samoa, his book *Leaves of the Banyan Tree* won the 1980 New Zealand Book Awards. He has also been awarded the Order of New Zealand.

Epeli Hau'ofa was one of the Pacific's most influential academics and writers. Born in Papua New Guinea in 1939 to Tongan missionary parents, he spent his later years teaching at the University of the South Pacific in Fiji. He was the author of numerous books, essays and poetry.

Notable Solomon Islands writers include John Saunana and Celo Kulagoe.

Albert Wendt, after his investiture as a Member of the Order of New Zealand

# European Writers

The islands of the Pacific have inspired many writers. American writer, James A. Michener, travelled around the South Pacific islands with the navy. He went on to set a number of books in the region, his most famous being *South Pacific*, which was turned into a film and successful Broadway musical.

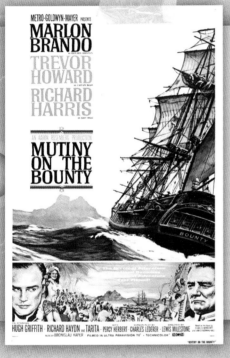

Charles Nordhoff and James Hall were writers who met at the end of World War I, when they collaborated on a book. Nordhoff suggested that they move to the South Pacific to work on books together.

They both married Tahitian women and worked on their own books, before collaborating on a novel that would bring lasting success, *Mutiny on the Bounty*.

The book was turned into a film starring Marlon Brando. They went on to write two sequels, to complete the series known as *The Mutiny Trilogy*.

Robert Louis Stevenson, author of *Treasure Island* and *Kidnapped*, called Samoa home. His travel writing and essays are an important historical contribution to 19th century life in the Pacific. He is buried at the top of Samoa's Mt Vaea, and his former home is a museum.

Robert Louis Stevenson with Princess Liliuokalani, sovereign monarch of Hawaii, c. 1889

# GLOSSARY

**atoll** ring-shaped coral reef or island

**climate change** shift in the planet's weather and climate patterns

**deforestation** clearing and destruction of large areas of trees

**ethnic** from a different culture or country

**independence** when a country is ruled by its own people

**Mariana Trench** deepest point on earth

**Pacific Ring of Fire** geographical area in the Pacific Ocean where earthquakes and volcanoes are common

# INDEX

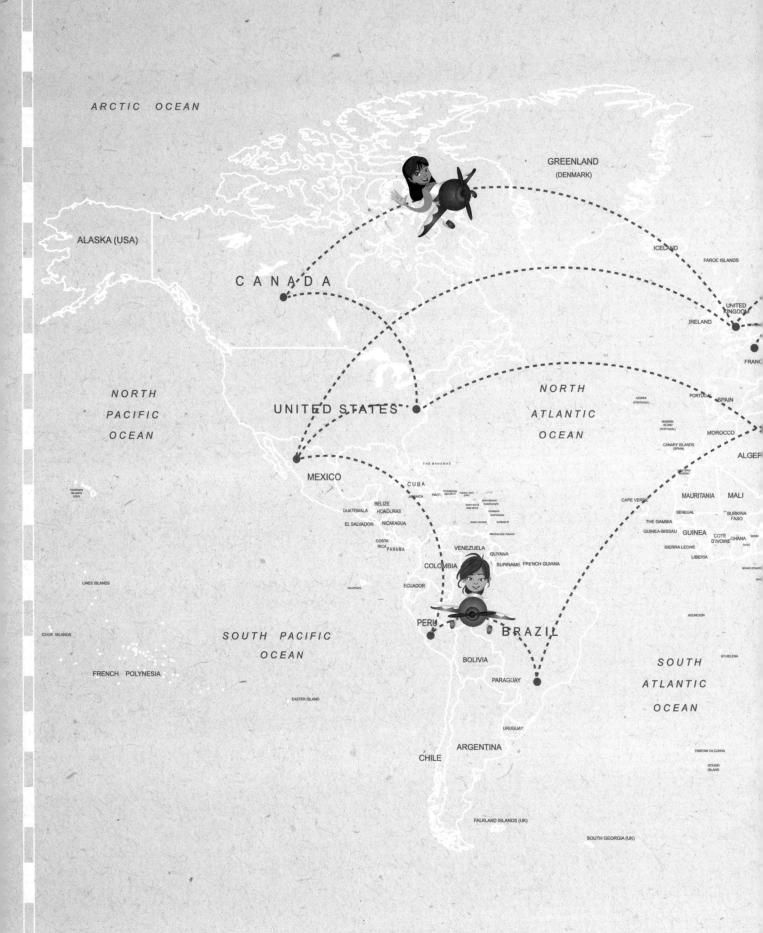